12

LONDON BOROUGH OF LEWISHAM

LIBRARY SERVICE

Author

Title

Books or discs must be returned on or before the last date stamped on label or on card in book pocket. Books or discs can be renewed by telephone, letter or personal call unless required by another reader. After library hours use the Ansafone Service (01-698 7347). For hours of opening and charges see notices at the above branch, but note that all lending departments close at 1 pm on Wednesday and all libraries are closed on Sundays, Good Friday, Christmas Day, Bank Holidays and Saturdays prior to Bank Holidays.

...one Service after

...s - 01-698 7347

...rned on or before ''
...or discs ...
...th...

2.

KEY DISCUSSION BOOK 2

Advertising

DENIS THOMAS

Published by
LONGMAN GROUP LIMITED
in association with
THE INSTITUTE OF ECONOMIC AFFAIRS

LONGMAN GROUP LIMITED
London
Associated companies, branches and representatives
throughout the world.

First published May 1965, by
The Institute of Economic Affairs
2, Lord North Street, Westminster, London, S.W.1.
Second edition, revised, 1969.
Published by LONGMAN GROUP LTD.
SBN 582 35053 0

Printed in Great Britain by
Rocastle Ltd., Leavesden, Watford, Herts.

Contents

FOREWORD

The Key Discussion Books were introduced by the Institute of Economic Affairs to provide texts for sixth-form or first-year college students and their teachers. The task of providing suitable material faces the special difficulty of serving minds in the process of changing from uncritical acceptance of school books as bibles to a gradual awakening to the impermanence of learning and the diverse approaches and judgements of scholars. The sixth-former and first-year student has begun to sense that the writers of textbooks are not infallible sources of eternal truths; the teacher must nurture this awakening critical faculty and show that it is the diversity of conflicting hypotheses that nourishes the mind and yields conclusions to be tested by argument and evidence.

The Key Discussion Books comprise 10,000 words divided into five sections of 2,000 words, accompanied by questions and readings. They are intended to present the broad essentials of their subject and to introduce the student to the economic analysis of public policy. They do not pretend to be comprehensive or definitive but are offered as up-to-date, documented and concise aids to teaching. They are on subjects of direct relevance to the A-level, technical college, and first-year university syllabuses in economics, but are also of wider interest to the student of public affairs, general knowledge or current history.

The Institute has been assisted in its selection of subjects, authors and timing by the members of its School Texts Advisory Panel (see inside front cover) to whom it expresses its gratitude.

No. 2 in the series is a study of advertising by Mr. Denis Thomas, B.A. (Oxon), an editor and writer with wide experience in journalism and television. He is the author of *Competition in Radio* (Occasional Paper 5, IEA, 1965) and of *Copyright and the Creative Artist* (Research Monograph 10, IEA, 1967), and compiler of an anthology for sixth form discussion groups, *Personal Opinion* (Nelson, 1963). He illustrates his review of the economic significance of advertising by statistical material not easily available in school texts, and draws on examples from recent advertising campaigns. For the second edition the Tables have been completely revised but the text remains substantially unaltered.

Authors have been asked to be objective in content and tone; personal judgements are not necessarily shared by the Institute or by the members of the Advisory Panel.

It is hoped that teachers and sixth formers will let us have their views on the content and method of the Key Books in order that we may take their suggestions and criticisms into account in subsequent numbers.

Arthur Seldon

1. The Purpose of Advertising

IF IT were possible, by means of a time machine, to transfer oneself into any country or any society at an earlier stage in its history, what would be the signs by which the time-traveller would know where he was?

The visual impact of the place would be the first to strike him. Nature and all its works might not change so much from century to century as to mark any one period in time from another; but Man and his works would. There would be the physical evidence of how Man has made the world a more and more comfortable place for his own species to live in. There would be the presence or absence of roads, vehicles, buildings and feats of engineering. There would be the clothes and the manners and the outward behaviour of people. There would be the things they possessed and valued, the objects of art they admired, the pictures and symbols surrounding them in their daily lives.

Somewhere in the centre of this first visual impression there might be evidence of advertising. That is to say, objects or causes or public services would be plainly announced. The type of society these people lived in, and the quality of their lives – at least in a material sense – would be clearly reflected in the goods and services advertised, and the forms and appeals of the advertisements themselves. The more backward the society, the fewer such examples there would be; the more restricted their lives, the more austere the outward signs of information and persuasion.

The fact is, the obvious way to assess the outward and material state of a society at first glance is to look at what it has produced for itself by way of easing the strains and discomforts of life, substituting for them a whole range of aids and balms and mechanical time-savers. Obviously, this is not the only criterion, and perhaps it is not even the most important one: it may be less easy, for example, to gauge spiritual or cultural standards by looking for tangible evidence in this way.

We have coined a phrase for this: 'the standard of living'. It begs many questions, but it is a convenient tag. And right at the heart of it, at any rate in the western world, is the economic phenomenon we know as advertising.

Do we need advertising?

Anyone who has ever asked himself the question 'do we *need* advertising?' might start by considering what it would be like *not* to have it. If it had been possible for modern Man to keep advertising out of his life, we should probably not today be enjoying the benefits of the most advanced material civilisation the world has ever known. We might by now have developed the motor car, but would there be more than a poor selection of rather crude models to choose from? We might have learned to fly, but would there be much to fly in except military machines, which almost alone seem to develop without the stimulus of commercial competition? Would that widely maligned commodity, the detergent, ever have been developed to its present state of usefulness? Or might we still have to be content with yellow bar soap, and housewives with a scrubbing board?

TABLE I

ADVERTISING EXPENDITURE IN SELECTED COUNTRIES, 1966

Country	Currency	Total advertising expenditure	Expenditure as percentage of national income
Argentina	Pesos	44,550 m.	1·00
Belgium	Belgian Franc	7,414 m.	1·10
Canada	Canadian Dollar	765·6 m.	1·70
Ceylon	Rupees	31 m.	·44
Finland	Finnish Mark	444 m.	2·00
France	Franc	3,520 m.	·93
Ireland	Pound	6·9 m.	·8
Israel	Pound (Israeli)	48·7 m.	·57
Japan	Yen	383·1 bil.	1·36
Netherlands	Guilder	862 m.	1·39
Switzerland	Swiss Franc	1,351 m.	2·60
Turkey	Turkish Lira	194 m.	·32
U.K.	Pound Sterling	439 m.	1·50
U.S.A.	Dollar	16,601 m.	2·60

Source: International Advertising Association: *Advertising Investments Around the World*, 8th Biennial Report, December 1967.

In common with all statistics those in Table I must be regarded critically. In particular the categories into which the information is collected are not the same for all countries. For instance, the money spent on advertising in Canada does not include the cost of exhibitions, display, or point-of-sale material, and that in Finland covers cinema and television only. Similarly there are many differences between the figures of each country, and furthermore the estimates for the less developed countries are very crude. Nonetheless, they serve as a rough basis for comparison.

Warning: notice that the figures for the total expenditure per country are given in the currency of the country in question and are therefore not directly comparable. *Question:* are the figures in the last column roughly comparable?

Conditions like these are to be found in many countries which distrust the profit motive and thrust private enterprise underground (they never quite manage to extinguish it). There, the public are not enabled to exercise free choice in a consumers' market, and such homely demands as wanting to wear fully-fashioned stockings or use perfumed soap or run a cheap but stylish motor car must remain largely unsatisfied. In societies where wants like these are heeded, sooner or later somebody meets them – or tries to – by making and putting on the market an article for which he knows, or at any rate guesses, there will be a demand. Having made his article he has to sell it. To sell it he has to bring it to the attention of people. And to do that he has to resort to publicity in one or more of its many forms. (Table I.)

If the manufacturer is right, and people find his article useful or desirable and buy it in any quantity, competitors enter the market.[1] They too advertise, so as to give

[1] Patents and copyright may obstruct competition but they can seldom stop it altogether.

themselves a chance of getting into the market on equal terms. Before long six, ten or fifty manufacturers are all engaged in a similar activity – making and selling a commodity for which there is, for the time being at least, a proven demand. They compete in the same market, or, with the help of persuasion, introduce new customers to it and in that way expand the market as a whole.

Consumer benefits and dangers

In conditions like these the consumer may benefit in several ways. The keener the competition for his money, the more likely it is that the product itself will improve. Also, as often as not it will come down in price.

The dangers inherent in a free economy are commonly cited: waste, over-production of some things, under-production of other – sometimes more desirable – ones; duplication of research; dissipation of sales effort and so on. But the biggest danger of all is monopoly.[1] How to prevent it, while protecting the basic right to go into business for oneself, and having gone in to expand it, is a problem which has exercised economists and others on both sides of the Atlantic. But even a monopoly is liable to find itself with competitors. In central heating, for instance, the nationalised coal industry is in competition with the nationalised electricity industry, the nationalised gas industry and the private-enterprise oil industry. In turn all four are in competition with one another. The state monopolies, and the big private enterprise oil companies, advertise heavily. They each claim advantages for their own service. They all have substantial financial backing. They all claim that theirs is the best heating system. Strictly speaking, they can't all be right – but each may have advantages for different users. In the end it is the consumer himself who decides. He has a choice, and none of the powerful persuaders is in a strong enough position to influence him against his judgment for long at the expense of all the others.

One purpose of advertising is to build up consumer loyalty, as the advertisers call it. It is possible to make enough people believe in a product's excellence for it to reach a position of near-monopoly. When that happens, competing brands have the job of breaking its hold. This can be done by a concentrated campaign of salesmanship which may include, in addition to advertising, such devices as better packaging, price cutting, free gift offers and other inducements. An example of this kind of competition is to be found in the British tobacco industry. Two big combines share the bulk of the market, while retaining dozens of different brands of cigarettes under their respective banners – and the market remains open for the entry of new challengers. Even within the two large groups, individual brands are competing for popularity. Each has its own advertising 'image', and competing lines are regularly introduced into what looks – from the outside – like an already saturated market.

Current advertising campaigns at once call to mind other instances of this kind, and at this point it is useful to distinguish between a prejudice against certain *commodities* and a view on their *advertising*. Gambling – to take an obvious example – is not against the law. Nor is taking pills. So activities like these may be as freely advertised as alcoholic liquor, Moral Re-Armament, strip-clubs, horror films, the South African Government or the political parties, no matter how many people may disapprove of what some or all of them stand for.

[1]This is the subject of Key Discussion Book 1, *Monopoly and Competition*, by George Cyriax.

How advertising is used

Some of these examples suggest a kinship between advertising and propaganda. There is obviously a difference in *motive* between the textile firm of Courtauld, for instance, buying newspaper space to advertise a new fabric, and the same firm buying similar space to ward off a takeover bid by ICI (as happened in 1962). But there is no difference in *principle* between a manufacturer trying to sell his goods by advertising and trying – also by advertising – to keep his company from being swallowed up.

Advertising clearly applies quite as much to non-commercial causes and services as it does to business. While we are surrounded by invitations to spend our money, the savings movements are urging us to put some aside, the building societies are inviting us to invest it, and charities are imploring us to give it away. There is a limit to the amount of money available even to the richest of us. Not only are manufacturers competing among themselves for it, but powerful counter-pressures are exerted from all sides to try to draw it off in other directions. Persuasion, in fact, can be brought to bear on us for a 'good' cause no less than for a commercial one. Appeals for aid following a national disaster – earthquake, hurricane or flood – are one example. Organised charities and humanitarian causes such as the Cancer Research Fund and Oxfam use advertising methods and outlets to win public support. The Church takes space in local newspapers to advertise services and socials. Road safety campaigners use the techniques of mass persuasion to help cut the accident rate. Government departments are now the second largest spenders on advertising, with total outgoings of nearly £6 million a year (Table III).

Politicians use advertising to try to get themselves elected: they, too, and the parties behind them, use the instruments of persuasion to 'sell' themselves. In the end, political parties are judged on the performance of what they promise in advance. In this respect they are in the same position as manufacturers: if the performance does not match up to the publicity, the public is not likely to be taken in a second time.

The position, however, is not quite as simple as this, since advertising is only one of the instruments at the salesman's command. If direct persuasion fails, there are other methods he can try, such as gift coupon schemes, mail order sales promotion, direct selling (cutting out the retailer), bonus offers – giving away a face flannel or a plastic tulip with every packet – and so on. When a manufacturer resorts to free gifts he is in effect cutting his prices. The consumer is by that much better off – assuming, of course, that he really *wants* a face flannel or a plastic tulip!

Again, of the £500 million a year which is spent on all forms of advertising in Britain alone, a considerable proportion goes into helping to promote commodities which are not sold direct to the public. For example, the drug industry advertises to doctors, the makers of machinery advertise to industrialists and manufacturers, the publishers of text books advertise to schoolteachers and educational authorities, and so on through the enormous range of specialist goods and services which lie outside the normal limits of consumer choice, but which may affect the well-being of the country no less directly than the flow of consumer goods out of the factory and into the home.

Three familiar products, each presented in a deliberately arresting manner with the 'appeal' to the consumer dramatically emphasised: manliness (beer), warmth (drinking chocolate), sexual attraction (man's shirt).

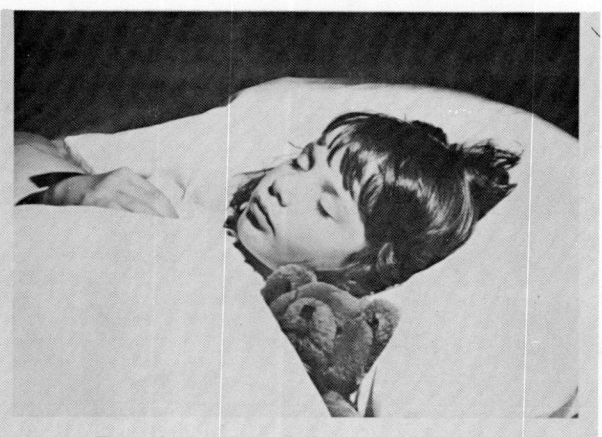

Family holiday? Go by sleeper!

Going on holiday this way is so easy you can do it with your eyes shut. You just lie back, close your eyes...and...you're there! Hundreds of miles vanish in sleep. The children love it. You get two extra days away. And it need only cost from 20/- each. A small price for the convenience and comfort (remember, you've no hotel bills to pay). For a holiday with a difference, take *your* family by sleeper this year.

Your modern sleeper is a bedroom on wheels	Network of over 100 Sleeper Services
■ Interior-sprung mattress ■ Crisp, fresh linen ■ Lashings of hot water ■ Large mirrors ■ Clothes hangers and plenty of luggage space ■ Wall to wall carpet ■ Morning tea and biscuits ■ Service only a bell-push away	Sleepers run the length and breadth of Britain, linking centre to centre and serving many distant tourist areas. Get the FREE Sleeper Services Colour Folder TODAY from any British Rail Station, Town Office or Appointed Travel Agent.

sleep as you go–overnight   **British Rail**

Does HOPE live at your address?

THE SAVE THE CHILDREN FUND

Patron : H.M. THE QUEEN

All the world loves a child, but in many places of the world today there are those who cannot give children their minimum needs for lack of money. Their hope is here. From many homes in this country, where unsatisfied hunger is unknown, money is spared to aid these children through the SCF and to bring them their long-term needs in welfare and education.

The SCF is your lifeline with the pitiful children you know you should help. You, although living thousands of miles away, can give a child the things he needs where his own mother is powerless to help. SCF clinics are ministering to the immediate needs of deserving children—providing food and relief, while thousands more, regardless of race, creed or colour, are being helped, through SCF welfare schemes, toward a future brighter and more promising than anyone could have expected.

Does hope live at your address? Will you help today's children to their human rights as tomorrow's citizens? Please send whatever you can with the donation form below.

THE SAVE THE CHILDREN FUND is working with THE FREEDOM FROM HUNGER CAMPAIGN

---- **DONATION FORM** ----

to: The Save the Children Fund
12 Upper Belgrave Street, London SW1

I enclose a donation to the Fund of .... £   s.   d.

NAME.. (Mr., Mrs., Miss or Title)
BLOCK CAPITALS THROUGHOUT
ADDRESS..
....

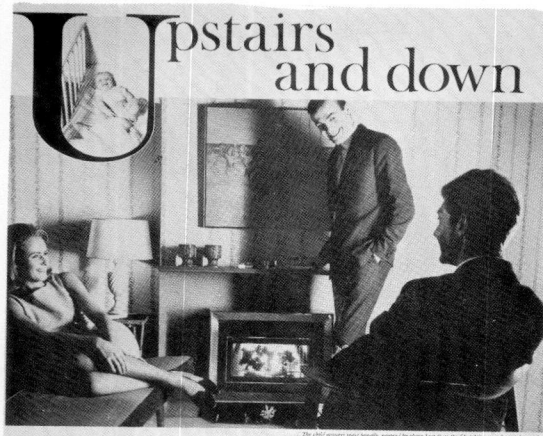

The child appears quite happily warmed by cheap heat from the Chatelaine room heater downstairs.

CHEAP HEAT
from one solid fuel room heater

HERE's proper heating, so cheap you can afford it earlier in life. And not just downstairs, but upstairs too! One handsome room heater, like the clean-lined Chatelaine shown above, with a high-output back boiler, can run 3 or 4 radiators (depending on their size), a hot towel rail and all your hot water. Makes your living room gayer too, with its modern, elegant design and the friendly glow of real firelight.

Techniques used in advertising consumer goods are freely used for other commodities and services. Here, the nationalised rail services, the nationalised coal industry, and a well-known charity all use the same image to attract sympathy for their advertisements: a baby

Questions

1. 'The keener the competition the more likely it is that the product itself will improve.' Find examples which (*a*) seem to support (*b*) seem to contradict this statement.

2. An example is given of how nationalised concerns compete with one another in central heating. Cut out examples of these advertisements and discuss which are the most persuasive.

3. Give examples of different 'images': two each of cigarettes, chocolates, cars, book publishers.

4. Which current advertisements seem to you the most persuasive in inducing people to *save* money instead of spending it?

5. Can you find an example of a 'good' advertisement for a product or cause which you dislike or disapprove of?

2. Advertising and Economics

ADVERTISING, as can now be seen, is an integral part of our economic life. Whatever form it may take, it is an attempt to make people *do* something which affects the working of the laws of supply and demand.

In earlier times, up to about the Middle Ages, this was not necessary, because men were not, in the modern sense, consumers. Most people worked for themselves, supplying the family's basic needs from their own produce or their own labour. Those who were rich – which through the ages has meant owning property and land – needed little persuasion to buy such extra comforts as would make life more enjoyable.

It was the enterprise of individuals that broke through this simple economic structure. Industrialised societies do not remain static: energetic and ambitious men began to move into the upper, privileged reaches and by their efforts acquired property and land. They formed what became known as the middle class, and ever since they have dominated the growth of Western societies. It was they who over the last 300 years set up as merchants and importers, theatre-owners and booksellers, professional specialists of all kinds. Soon they began to make their services known – by publishing the first newspaper advertisements.

These might be for books, wigs, entertainments, lotteries, patent medicines, silver-ware, spices or slaves. They were written in styles even more exaggerated and over-coloured than many popular advertisements of the present time. That there were also plenty of them can be seen from any journal printed in England during the 18th century. In 1759 Dr. Johnson noted that 'advertisements are now so very numerous that they are very negligently perused'. He was referring to advertisements addressed to sophisticated townsmen like himself: advertisements aimed at a wider public developed only a hundred years later.

As trade with the rest of the world increased, so more commodities flowed into the country. Importers, merchants and wholesalers began announcing their wares, and with the growth of popular newspapers during the 1890s came beginnings of a highly organised advertising industry. Its purpose was to spread news of commodities and, increasingly, to persuade people to take notice of one particular brand or variety. Rising wages, the growth of industrial towns and shorter working hours contributed to the public's interest in such commodities. With a rising standard of living came a desire for better things to eat, wear or furnish the home. Large-scale production depended on finding regular outlets and a widening market. Advertising – increasingly expert and specialised – stimulated sales, and sales stimulated competition; and all the time the range of choice was widening. Thus the 'mass market' was born.

Growth of the popular press

To win access to that market, many manufacturers set up their own selling organisa-tion, and went over the heads of wholesalers and shopkeepers by making themselves known direct to the public – by advertising. And of course they advertised where

TOTAL ADVERTISING EXPENDITURE IN THE UK IN 1938 TO 1967
(£ million)

	1938	1956	1963	1967
Press	51·1	158·6	234	282
Poster and Transport	5·3	15	16	18
Outdoor Signs	2·5	11	15	15
Television	—	10·6	85	124
Cinema	0·7	5·5	5	6
Catalogues, circulars, etc. ..	10	35	42	*
Window and Shop Displays ..	7·6	22·4	34	*
Exhibitions	6	11·5	17	*
Free samples and gifts	4	12·2	17	*
Miscellaneous[1]	5·4	6	9	2
Administration	5	21	27	—
TOTAL	98	309	501	447
Expenditure as a percentage of GNP	1·9	1·7	1·9	1·3
Expenditure as a percentage of Consumers' Expenditure ..	2·2	2·3	2·6	1·8
Expenditure as a percentage of Net National Income	2·0	1·8	2·1	1·5

Source: Advertising Expenditure and other estimates published by the Advertising Association.

[1]Includes radio advertising, novelties, printed bags, etc. (the figure of £2 million for 1967 covers radio advertising only).
Figures for these categories are no longer available.

What is the GNP in Table II? If 1.9% of GNP in 1938 and 1.7% of GNP in 1956 were spent on advertising, does it follow that the total amount spent in 1956 was less than that spent in 1938? Why do you think the total amount spent on film advertising declined in recent years (though it slightly increased in 1967)? Can you supply the missing figure for expenditure on television advertising for 1938? What sort of items would you expect to find included under the heading administration?

---

people would be most likely to see them or hear them, notably in the mass-circulation newspapers. (Tables II and III.)

Examples of firms which, early in their careers, chose to set up their own retailing organisations are the big chemists, like Boots and Timothy Whites, and grocers like Lipton's (originally a tea importer) and Home and Colonial. Many brewers sold direct to the public with their 'tied' public houses. An exception was Guinness: they relied on advertising to get their stout into other brewers' pubs by sheer pressure of public demand. The Co-operative Societies still sell a wide range of their own brands. So do big chain stores like Marks and Spencer.

In Britain, politicians did once try to curb the growth of a free press by imposing a

TABLE III

THE TOP TWENTY ADVERTISERS IN 1967

Advertiser	Total £
Unilever	14,840,700
Government Departments	5,801,900
Cadbury Group	5,497,000
Mars Group	5,267,600
Reckitt & Colman	4,845,400
Procter & Gamble	4,585,600
Beecham Group	4,159,700
Imperial Tobacco	3,985,200
Gallaher	3,948,600
Heinz	2,338,500
Brooke Bond	2,101,400
Rowntree	2,023,500
Kellogg	1,881,100
Spillers	1,834,400
Carreras	1,129,100
Milk Marketing Board	1,759,100
British Leyland Motors	1,683,600
ICI	1,643,800
Nestlé	1,585,600
Colgate-Palmolive	1,524,300

Source: Media Expenditure Analysis Ltd. supplement to *Advertisers Annual 1968.*

Unilever and Procter & Gamble are the principal manufacturers of soap and detergent products. Reckitt & Colman make household, pharmaceutical, toilet and food products. Mars, in addition to making a wide range of sweets and chocolates, are also leading manufacturers of pet-food. The Beecham Group manufacture pharmaceuticals, soft drinks, haircream, toothpaste and other domestic products.

What are the most famous brands produced by these big companies? Can you think of similar products, not so widely advertised as theirs, which are 'just as good'?

Government Departments are now the second biggest advertisers. Is this a waste of public money? Is there a difference between Government advertising and any other kind?

---

tax of one shilling on all published advertisements. That was in 1712, and it quickly lead to the failure of many journals including the *Spectator*. Even in those days, of the nine daily newspapers being published in London, no fewer than five were primarily advertising sheets, and the other four devoted at least half their space to advertising. The tax was finally abolished in 1853, and from that year dates the growth of popular journalism as we know it today.

The growth of the press, therefore, owes much to the development of mass advertising. To this day most newspapers depend on advertisements for their existence:

TABLE IV

ADVERTISING EXPENDITURE ON MAIN MEDIA RELATED TO NATIONAL INCOME IN SELECTED COUNTRIES, 1966

Country	Expenditure (U.S. $ millions)	As % of National Income	Expenditure per capita U.S. $
U.S.A.	10,977	1·77	55·5
Australia	320	1·59	27·8
Canada	535	1·33	27·3
Germany (West)	1,222	1·35	20·7
United Kingdom ..	1,053	1·48	19·6
Netherlands	147	0·85	11·9
Austria	72	0·92	10·0
Japan	940	1·21	9·9
Spain	212	1·13	6·7
Argentina	133	0·82	6·0
Portugal	36	1·21	4·0

Source: The Advertising Association, 1968. Expenditure included is that on Press, television, radio, cinema, posters and outdoor.

All figures, except for the U.K., are taken from *Advertising Investments Round the World,* December 1967, published by the I.A.A., New York.
Figures in national currencies have been converted to U.S. $ at the official exchange rates of end-1967. Comparable figures for Switzerland and Sweden were not available when this table was compiled: both these countries would otherwise figure in the table.

---

without this source of revenue they would soon go out of business, since the cost of producing a popular paper far exceeds revenue from sales. For example, the last Royal Commission on the Press[1] found that a reader who paid 3d. for a copy of a popular paper received an article which had cost 4½d. to produce and distribute. The balance, including a margin for profit, had to come out of advertisement revenue. Costs keep rising – labour, materials, editorial expenses such as air fares and telephone charges – but if a paper tries to increase its revenue by putting its price up it risks a drop in sales. That in turn could mean less advertisements, less advertisements mean fewer pages, fewer pages mean losing readers; and so the economic spiral continues.

The freedom of the press, its independence from political pressures, is possible because its main source of income is advertising, mostly by 'business'. This in its turn could be nearly as dangerous, in some situations, as state domination such as exists in Cuba, Spain or most of Eastern Europe. But the danger is minimised by the fact that, in Great Britain, there is a multiplicity of newspapers of all shades of opinion – and a wide variety of advertising. The newspapers' collective vigilance over public affairs may often be an embarrassment to governments and prominent public figures, but it is safeguarded so long as there remains a wide choice.

[1]Cmnd. 1812, HMSO, 1962.

The real threat to a free press in Britain is the declining number of newspapers, though advertising has a disproportionate influence on the *economics* of newspaper publishing. Dependence on advertisements does affect editorial attitudes of some newspapers. For instance, it would not be in a popular newspaper's financial interest to wage an editorial campaign against a very large firm which was also a big press advertiser. The papers most sensitive to advertising 'pressure' are those which are struggling for circulation: they cannot afford to make powerful commercial enemies, or to turn down advertising offered in exchange for editorial 'co-operation' – such as including publicity matter disguised as a news story or a feature. Successive Royal Commissions on the Press have failed to produce any workable answer to this dilemma.

Brand names and mass markets

Once advertising had begun to concentrate on branded goods, commodities became familiar through the name on the label. Whereas in the past it had been largely left to the wholesaler or shopkeeper to judge what goods to stock and to sell them 'loose', there grew up a pressure from outside – from his own customers – to stock particular brands of packaged goods. This was a direct first effect of the advertising of such brands in newspapers or magazines, on walls or fences, or on public transport. By this means the manufacturers began to break the hold of the wholesalers and retailers and obliged them to display their brands.

Soon another characteristic of modern society had begun to assert itself: mass production. The Industrial Revolution released a flood of goods made by new methods and new machinery – goods which had to be sold in huge quantities if the benefits of cheap processing were to be passed on to the public. Advertising was enlisted to make such commodities household words. Once, there was a useful, if variable and crude, commodity known simply as 'soap'. In the 50 years following the lifting of the advertising tax, it became closely identified with such names as Pear's and Hudson's, Sunlight, Fairy and Wright's Coal Tar. Consumption soared. Similarly with cigarettes: as brand names became household words so their popularity grew. Before long, taxes from tobacco amounted to such a huge item that smoking became one of the Exchequer's mainstays in balancing the Budget.[1]

The time of the great advertising break-through in the last century and early years of this one was, like all revolutionary periods of history, a time of roguery and profiteering on a wide scale. Claims for cure-alls were made with cynical exaggeration, competitors' goods were vilified, quacks and mountebanks abounded. Even big firms were tempted into mass deception.

As the public became better educated and more critical – and the law more vigilant – so the cruder claims were toned down and less strident methods of persuasion took their place. Celebrities were offered sums of money if they would endorse a product. At first, elegant figures from 'society' were used to bring added allure in this way, as with toilet commodities of various kinds. But 'society' means much less to our present-day egalitarian generation, and snob-appeal of this cruder kind is diminishing. Today, the face in the advertisement is more likely to be that of a television personality,

[1] Nearly £1,000 million in 1968.

a sporting celebrity or a popular comedian. The advertising men, ever sensitive to social change, have developed new ways of getting our attention.

Questions

1. Discuss the statement that the enterprise of individuals will always break through rigid class structures. Can you think of any examples in recent times?

2. Do you agree with Dr. Johnson's remark made 200 years ago that there are now so many advertisements that 'they are only negligently perused'? Which advertisements can be read purely for pleasure, if any?

3. List as many products as you can think of at home which were bought as a result – even indirectly – of an advertisement.

4. Give examples of products which (i) you buy regularly without the reminder of advertising, and (ii) which you have resisted buying because you do not like the way they are advertised.

5. In what sense does the press depend on advertising? Would you be prepared to pay double the price for a copy of your newspaper or favourite weekly magazine if it contained no advertisements at all?

3. Advertising in Action

IT WOULD be a very rash man who claimed that he was totally immune from the effects of advertising. We all like to think we are sales-resistant. But there is hardly an article in our homes, or in our pockets, that has not got there in some way because we have been *persuaded* to buy it. It is probable that the house or flat we live in first came to our notice through an advertisement. Many people owe their jobs to an announcement in the Situations Vacant column of a newspaper. Some people have even found themselves husbands or wives by the same method!

If we have a cold or a sore throat or a headache we call at a chemists and ask for pills or powders. We know what to ask for, because the makers of these medicines have impressed on us the merits of their products. But of course we do not buy X's pills or Y's powders just because the advertisements have told us to – the likelihood is that we or our family or friends tried them once before, and they seemed to live up to what was claimed for them. So next time we needed them we asked for the same brand.

In this simple illustration lies a basic truth about advertising: it can make people buy once, perhaps, but if the product does not come up to expectations advertising alone usually won't work a second time. The advertisers know this. Being professional businessmen themselves, they know that what has to be sold is the *quality* of the commodity or service. Manufacturers have mostly more sense than to spend much money trying to sell a new product which is inferior to ones already on the market. The more they spend on advertising it, the more they are likely to lose money in the end – because sooner or later the public will find them out.

One of the arguments put forward in defence of big firms is that they have a good name to protect: any article bearing their label carries with it their reputation for quality and value, and if one widely advertised line of theirs proves to be inferior, their whole range suffers by the loss of trust and goodwill which results. The argument seems to hold water, but it is difficult to prove. Very often, with the help of heavy advertising which makes possible large-scale production, such a commodity is cheaper than its competitors. A sound assumption for the consumer is that within the limits of his shopping sense he can expect to get no more than his money's worth.

How an advertising agency works

Increasingly, people with things to sell employ advertising agencies to help put them across to the public. Today, nearly 60 per cent of the total expenditure on advertising in Britain is placed by such agencies for their clients. These clients vary from small manufacturers in highly specialised markets to government departments and political parties. We have already considered the wide range of goods, services, political parties, and causes which use advertising methods. To them must now be added *Which?*, the consumer research journal that reports independently on the comparative merits of branded goods and increasingly uses advertising to recruit new subscribers.

Advertising agencies vary enormously in size, organisation and scope, from small

TABLE V

VARIATIONS IN ADVERTISING COSTS AS A PROPORTION OF 'TURNOVER' (t) OR RETAIL PRICE (r.p.)

Product				Percentage
Cooper's aerosols	..	..	t	10-15
Which?	..	..	t	10·0
Instant coffee powders	..	..	t	9·6
Cadbury snack	..	..	t	9·0
Persil	..	..	r.p.	5-8
Blue Band margarine	..	..	r.p.	6·0
Harveys wines	..	..	t	4·0
Bird's Eye frozen foods	..	..	t	4·0
Schweppes soft drinks	..	..	t	3·5
Renault Dauphine	..	..	r.p.	2
Mobilgas petrol	..	..	r.p.	1·3
Guinness stout	..	..	r.p.	1·2
Heinz baby foods	..	..	t	1·0
Shell and Esso petrol	..	..	r.p.	0·05
Milk	..	..	r.p.	0·3
Industrial coal	..	..	r.p.	0·04

Source: Harris and Seldon, *Advertising and the Public*, IEA, 1962, p. 59.

Table V should be read as follows: The manufacturers of Cooper's aerosols spent 10-15% of turnover (t) on advertising their products. For every packet of Blue Band margarine that is purchased 6% of the retail price (r.p.) is due to advertising costs.

Many factors affect the percentage of the cost per week which is due to advertising any particular product. Make a list of some of them. Would you expect the proportion to be constant, or to vary with the scale of manufacture and other conditions? Does this Table tell you anything about the total expenditure on advertising of any of the products listed?

---

ones with perhaps half-a-dozen people on the staff to ones whose names and services are internationally known and who handle accounts running into millions of pounds a year. Most large agencies will not normally take on a new account unless the client intends to spend at least £20,000 regularly each year. The agencies are paid by commission: they take a percentage of the client's outlay, in the form of a rebate (generally 15 per cent) payable by the newspaper, magazine or other 'medium' in which advertisement space is sold. Some economists criticise the commission system as being rigid and restrictive. Some critics of advertising (and some advertising men) say the commission system is wasteful, because it appears to be in the agencies' financial interest to persuade their clients to spend more and more money on advertising, as opposed to other ways of selling.

The advertising agencies, like everybody else in the business world, are out to make profits. Their individual turnover is liable to violent fluctuation, caused by ups and downs in business or the acquisition or withdrawal of accounts. As a profession, advertising is to this extent basically unstable. Significantly, perhaps, most of the biggest advertising organisations remain private companies: you can't buy shares in them. (Table VII, page 28, shows the largest agencies in 1967.)

Let us take a brief look at how a modern agency might tackle a full-scale advertising campaign for a new client. First it would satisfy itself that the client had the financial means to support a campaign on the scale envisaged. Then it would conduct its own research into the product to be advertised and the market that might possibly be opened up for it. Sometimes the new product might be a potential competitor of one of the agency's existing accounts; in such a case the agency would think hard before taking it on. If it felt this would jeopardise either the new product's chances or those of the present one, it would probably turn the account down.

If it decided to go ahead, the next step would be to test the market by consumer research, collecting information on all competing lines, scrutinising trade papers for pointers and so on. If the product were one which was to be sold direct to the consumer – such as household goods – various experimental packages might be tried and members of the public invited to pass opinions on it. A study of retailing and other forms of distribution would follow to decide what part of the marketing effort should be devoted to a sales force, window displays, special offers, trade terms, and other methods of drawing attention. (Table V, page 17, shows specimen advertising costs.)

Then would come the allocation of advertising space – or in the case of television, advertising time. For some products, national advertising in the mass-circulation papers probably produces the best results even at the cost of, say, £2,000 for a half page. For others, selected journals with a specialised readership offer a better return for the advertiser's money. If a 'commercial' specially made for television is considered the most economic means of bringing it to people's notice, there is still a choice between 30-second 'spots' at peak viewing time on the national network costing perhaps £4,000 and more frequent 15-second 'spots' on local stations costing as little as £20. Alternative or supplementary methods might include posters, cinema slides, direct mailings to potential customers, competitions with big prizes – all of which have merits for particular products. (Table IV, page 13, shows media costs.)

During the earlier stages the campaign might be confined to one or two selected areas, to test the public's reaction. If the tests are encouraging, the full programme can be launched on a wider scale.

Obviously, not all advertising campaigns of this kind are on behalf of new products: as often as not, it is an existing manufacturer who is anxious to re-assert his product's claims by advertising that often seems monotonously repetitive, to hold his own in face of rising competition, or to remind his own customers that he is still very much in business. Habits change, and the manufacturer who falls behind the times is often hard put to it to catch up. Even layout and typography – the province of the agency's art department – must be kept up to date. Some apparently old-fashioned labels which may be thought too well-known to risk modernising are allowed to stay much as they were twenty or even fifty years ago, such as Tate and Lyle's Golden Syrup, Camp Coffee, and Holbrook's Worcestershire Sauce. There are some products with well-known names one never seems to see advertised; but the vast majority are constantly kept before us in one or more of a variety of ways, including simply display on shop counters. Thus they remind us of their continued existence, making no new claims, perhaps, but steadily keeping themselves in the public eye.

In all this, advertising is regarded as an integral part of salesmanship in its broadest sense. It is closely involved in packaging, distribution, display – what the trade calls marketing and merchandising–and without its selling function it has no other purpose.

Detergents and the housewife

For an example of how advertising can help revolutionise some aspects of daily life, let us take a look at one of the most controversial and widely discussed examples, synthetic detergents. First, it must be plain that they are a mass product: they are bought frequently by practically everybody, and they are known by name even to people who do not buy them regularly. When they first made their appearance, the washing and washing-up were done with old-fashioned soap and soda or at best with soap powders. These were universal, tried and trusted methods of doing an everyday job. The makers of synthetic detergents – chemically-prepared powders which dissolve grease rapidly – had to convince housewives that their new product was even better.

To do so they set up an advertising clamour which has not abated by one decibel since it started. They discovered by market research that the housewife's instinctive test of cleanliness was whiteness, so they seized on that as their first selling point. The message had to be plain and simple to the point of idiocy: detergents washed white, or whiter than white, or whitest of all. A continuing mass market was essential if the product – a result of costly research and chemical engineering – was to be sold at a competitive price. In 1948, when detergents first came on the market, there were several hundred brands, many produced on an inefficient scale and therefore expensive or of low quality. Since then, competition for the majority market has knocked out all the smaller ones: three or four big firms now have the major share of the market between them.

These firms claim that there is still enough competition between the giants to keep the price down and that the product is constantly being improved. And if it should be asked why, now that everyone buys detergents, they are still advertised so widely, the makers' answer is threefold. They say, first, that to stop advertising is to risk an immediate drop in sales. Second, they say the market is continually changing: 400,000 newly-wedded housewives join it every year. Third, they claim that, though the product is continually being improved, successful mass selling enables them to keep the price down despite the steadily rising cost of living.

In 1966 the Board of Trade brought pressure on the two main detergent manufacturers – Lever Brothers and Procter & Gamble – to sell some of their leading brands without the built-in 'expense' of heavy advertising, and to offer the public more contents per packet instead. The two firms did so, and switched their advertising to brands which actually contained less powder than the non-advertised ones. *Which?* reported that there was virtually no difference between the quality of the powders, and named the non-advertised varieties as 'best buys'. Yet it quickly became apparent that housewives were buying the advertised brands in far larger quantities than the 'bargain' brands: confirmation, as the marketing men see it, that people do not necessarily put value for money above all other considerations when they go shopping. The experience also points to one of the main purposes of advertising in the mass market – developing 'brand loyalty'.

Marketing ventures of this kind are closely watched by rival firms; for in the world of mass production and marketing there is always the threat of a competitor stealing a march, or of an old adversary taking on a new lease of life (sometimes because he has taken on a new advertising agency), or one of those sudden inexplicable swings of the national mood which from time to time make nonsense of the advertising man's slide-rule calculations.

Advertising's success—and failures

All around us there are examples of highly-advertised products which have passed into daily use: instant coffee, silicone polish, electric shavers (though the old hot-water-and-shaving-brush variety has made a successful come-back by clever advertising of improved razor blades), mini-cars, ballpoint pens. In nearly every case such products are evidently considered by large numbers of people as efficient, or time-saving, or in some way beneficial in a society advancing towards more leisure and a higher standard of living. But, to repeat a point made earlier, articles like these are not the offspring of advertising: ultimately they sell and are used because in various ways they meet people's wants. Advertising has helped them penetrate into very many homes, but in the end it is their intrinsic qualities of usefulness, value, or mere novelty which have made them popular.

No less noteworthy are the advertising industry's failures. Not even the heavy spending of advertisers and clever copy-writing of the agencies could convert us to drinking instant tea: most of us prefer to make it the old, slow way – the *proper* way, as most people obstinately think (unlike instant coffee, a market in which no long-standing national drinking habit has to be overcome). Similarly, an American invader of the British domestic market was sent back home wiser – and poorer – after failing to convert the British housewife to the all-in-one cake mix. Confident of a sweeping success, the makers embarked on a nation-wide advertising campaign. They kept it up for three years and spent a million dollars. Then they acknowledged defeat: British housewives, they found, like to bake their cakes the way their mothers taught them – with no short cuts, no 'cheating'.

Again, the experienced Beecham Group a few years ago introduced a new hair shampoo with a method of application different from the conventional bottle or the newer sachet. A test campaign yielded promising results, and in 1957 and 1958 about £150,000 was spent on a national advertising campaign, mainly on television. In six months the new shampoo became the biggest seller in its field. Then sales began to fall, and within three years dropped by 75 per cent. Beecham discontinued the shampoo. Its failure was simply that, once the novelty wore off, women returned to the conventional brands. Heavy advertising had persuaded them to *try* it for a time, but it could not persuade them to *change* to it.

Building a 'prestige' image

While we are considering the functions of advertising it will be as well to take into account some of the less obvious ones. Of these, perhaps 'prestige' advertising is the most interesting example. Here, a firm or organisation seems to be concerned to project a suitable 'image' of itself rather than to sell its product. The advertisement might take the form of a large, well-photographed picture expressive of the dignity or sophistication or sense of humour on which the advertiser likes to pride himself, accompanied by a line or two telling the reader that his is an old, worthy firm, or a brilliant new one, and little more.

The usefulness of this kind of advertising cannot be calculated from the balance sheet, perhaps, but it is by no means as uncommercial as it might appear. The conscious 'image-making' aspect of advertising is a comparatively recent development but is now often part of a firm's marketing system. A prestige advertisement, repeated at discreet intervals in the so-called 'quality' newspapers and journals, can have the effect of inducing a sympathetic public attitude to the firm. To what purpose? It might attract investors looking for a safe, likeable company to buy shares in; or it might commend itself to young men of calibre looking for a respected or prestigious firm to work for; or again it might have at least half an eye on its own employees, who like to see their firm making a pleasing public impression and who might as a result take a more sympathetic attitude towards it in the event, say, of a wages dispute. But here again, the advertiser must beware what claims he makes: an industrial firm which claimed in public advertisements that it was one big happy family, when its own employees knew it was seething with discontent, would only humiliate itself by buying space to proclaim a patent untruth. Or, to take a famous example which shows that prestige advertising cannot always manipulate public feeling: ICI spends large sums on prestige advertising, but this did not prevent a wave of public antagonism towards it when it tried its spectacular take-over of Courtaulds. As we have noted already, Courtaulds took advertising space to urge their share-holders to stand firm.

In all these ways, the persuaders are occupied in catching our attention and planting a message in our minds – often, they claim, in our subconscious minds. Even if you never read a newspaper or watch television, or if you travel on buses and trains with your eyes shut, you are bound to be aware of the assault on your attention. But the visible persuaders, as we might call them, are themselves exposed to counter-per-suasion: the best they can hope for is to address most of us most of the time. The effect is of discord rather than of chorus. It is up to us how much of it we take in or reject.

Questions

1. Do you trust branded goods more or less than anonymous ones? Give examples and say why.

2. Find a 'prestige' advertisement which seems to you to be doing its job well. Discuss its layout, language and 'message'. In what ways do you think the advertiser might benefit from such an advertisement?

3. Can you think of a private firm or nationalised industry you would like to join when you start work, on the strength – in part – of its nationally-advertised 'image'?

4. Can you see any difference between the 'images' of the three main political parties, as reflected in their publicity? Discuss the two examples of political advertising illustrated on p. iii.

5. Find examples of unsupportable claims made by commercial or political advertisers, for example by exaggeration, deceptive over-simplification, or suggestion.

4. The Techniques of Persuasion

IN THE free economy such as exists to various degrees in most western countries, manufacturers are seeking to meet people's wants. These may be basic, like a home or financial security, good health, insurance against sickness or old age. Or they may be more superficial, like wanting to be in the fashion by wearing the latest clothes or hairstyles.

In the world of business, advertising exists to further the sale of goods and services which meet human wants. If it is thought proper for house agents, say, to advertise properties for sale – described in the most attractive terms so as to catch the attention of the prospective customer – then it must be equally proper for a manufacturer of cosmetics or blue jeans or bubble gum to do the same. It is understandable, and indeed desirable, for most of us to suspect any special pleader of exaggeration, although much of the antagonism towards advertising as an activity is entangled, as we briefly noted earlier, with people's feelings about the products themselves.

To take an extreme example, a staunch member of the Labour Party might consider that the Conservative Party's advertisements are misleading or downright false. Equally, a strong Tory supporter might regard Labour's advertisements as specious or inaccurate. And Liberals might be critical of both. In such cases, it is not really the advertisement that is under criticism: it is the product – or in this case the political cause – which the advertisement publicises. Similarly with advertisements for banishing bad breath or body odour: one's dislike of the mere notion is likely to set up an antagonistic attitude to the advertisement.

Giving products additional appeal

Human wants are what manufacturers, politicians and advertisers all seek to fathom and understand. Some wants, as we have just indicated, are simple enough; but many defy even the most ingenious market research. An organisation with something to sell cannot be at all certain that it will 'go' when it is put to the real test in the market unless by sheer chance or inspiration it turns out to be exactly what a lot of people suddenly find they have been wanting all the time.

More often, a product or brand has to make its way against entrenched competition. The result is that goods and service are 'sold' to us as being better, newer, cheaper (or dearer), smarter, or sexier than similar ones already on the market. Often, they are presented as carrying some kind of mystique: if you use a certain toothpaste you will make more friends because your smile will be brighter; if you use a certain perfume your true love will come tumbling into your arms; and so on. These suggestions are not usually put over too crudely; they are implied in the advertisement, either as pictures or as text, or sometimes in the name chosen for the commodity itself.

It does not follow that the articles themselves are bogus. They may very well be no less efficient and desirable than others on the market; but in such cases the advertiser has chosen a known human want or sentiment which may be 'good' or

TABLE VI

EXAMPLES OF VARYING COSTS OF ADVERTISING MEDIA, 1968

The cost for television is for a 30-second[1] showing at peak rates calculated per 1,000 homes. The press rates are calculated on the basis of a full-page advertisement per 1,000 circulation.[2]

Independent Television	13s. to 17s.
Daily Mirror, Daily Mail, Sunday Express, Women ..	13s. to 21s.
Homes & Gardens, Punch, Good Housekeeping, Flair, Family Circle	40s. to 50s.
Guardian, Observer, Vogue, Illustrated London News	£3 to £5
The Times, Country Life	£5 to £7
Financial Times	£10 plus

Source: British Rate & Data, May 1968.

[1]The decision to compare a 30-second showing with the cost of a full page is arbitrary. A 15- or 60-second period might as well have been chosen.
[2]Advertising rates depend less on circulation than on the size and quality of the readership. For a weekly or monthly journal the readership may be five or ten times as high as the circulation.

Table VI compares the costs of advertising in various well-known media. The cost is therefore calculated per 1,000 readers or homes. The figures quoted are based on rates for black-and-white advertisements. Costs for colour advertising in the press would be at least 50% more.

Why do costs vary so much? Is it true that the more you pay per 1,000 readers or homes, the better response you get? Or does it depend on what you are trying to sell? Would you advertise a record by a new pop-singer in the *Financial Times*? Where would you advertise it? Where would you advertise: (a) frozen food, (b) typewriters, (c) model gowns, (d) books on economics, (e) teenage clothes, (f) an encylopædia (g) Insurance for private medical services? (Why do you think the of the NHS are services not advertised?)

'bad' – companionship, ambition, success, envy, pride, prejudice, romance – and pinned his appeal to it rather than to the chemical or technical advantages his product may have over its competitors.

There are many examples in present-day advertisements which make this point clearly. Some brands of chocolates are presented as glamorous, the kind you eat sprawled on the floor while listening to the hi-fi. The chocolates themselves, needless to say, are just chocolates: the different 'images' are solely in the packaging, the brand names chosen for them, and the advertising 'message'.

Again, some cigarettes are advertised as a mark of sophistication and wordliness, while others are suggested as the kind you puff while laying bricks or driving a ten-ton truck. The tobacco is much the same: all manufacturers claim to use only the choicest leaf. But the 'want' is different. There are examples of products changing their whole personality by skilled use of this technique: the humble Oxo cube, for instance, has risen in the world from being a hard-up housewife's standby to the status of a middle-class bride's secret recipe for giving her husband's meals 'man appeal'.

Advertisers' methods of persuasion have in recent years used our ever-widening knowledge of the subconscious. There is now a better understanding of what lies in our subconscious minds, so that manufacturers can get goods on the market which in our *conscious* minds we may not even know we want. Where once an advertiser might have made an inspired guess at the kind of appeal that will strike home, today he can draw on established psychology to reinforce his insight. Perhaps we all secretly crave to live longer, or to emigrate to Tahiti, or to write a best-selling novel. If we do, sooner or later a brand of sweets will appear hinting at an unwrinkled old age, or a tobacco that will transport us to a Pacific island, or a shaving lotion that will catapult us into the Book of the Month class.

Is advertising good economics?

By appealing to us in this way – usually more subtly than in these hypothetical examples – the advertisers have succeeded (even unintentionally) in advancing our material standard of living. They have helped to make 'keeping up with the Joneses' a driving force of modern life. Is this a desirable thing? And, desirable or not, is it good economics?

This question turns on our attitude to advertising as an instrument of a free economy, in which no-one is restrained (except by specific laws) from selling his wares and in which rewards depend on satisfying the consumer. Advertisers can hardly be blamed for helping to form habits in us which we have come to enjoy – or for breaking habits that have stopped us from trying something new. Who can say that he really enjoyed his first swim, or his first cigarette, or getting into the habit of brushing his teeth twice a day, or his first attempt at driving a car? Each of these is 'artificial' if considered in terms of basic human wants. The wants have been created for us. Or were they there all the time, waiting for the pressures of commercialism and social change to bring them to the surface?

Again, we can see the working of human wants in the world of fashion. Skirt lengths rise and fall, or are made to rise and fall, by the mysterious rites of the women's fashion designers; but women are not the only ones to feel regular desires for change. In recent years, young men throughout the Western world have acquired an entirely new dress sense – fancy trimmings on jackets, tighter trousers, pointed shoes and so on. It was not the advertisers who brought about this sartorial revolution – which has now reached behind the Iron Curtain where advertising (except by the state) is generally not allowed. It began as a shift in public taste, by a minority in one world-wide section of male society, and became big business when manufacturers sensed it and catered for it.

Advertising, then, is largely engaged either in stimulating human wants or in seeking to meet them. Its techniques can be emotional or suggestive, or both. It is advertising of this kind which is most commonly accused of misrepresentation or dishonesty.

Giving the facts about a product

Would the alternative – mere 'factual' advertising – be more acceptable? To begin with, what are 'facts'? Who decides what is shining, unambiguous truth and what is not? Facts can be selective, and as such tell less than the truth. It may be a 'fact' that certain skin creams are made from whale oil, or contain hormones from a dead pig. Such facts alone, boldly stated, will not necessarily commend those particular brands to women customers. It may be a 'fact' that a certain brand of cigarette really is made of 'pure Virginia tobacco'; but it is hardly relevant for the advertiser to add the additional fact that it is nevertheless just as likely as any other brand to

CONSERVATIVES give you a better standard of living

don't chuck it away!

After 13 years of Conservative failure, Britain urgently needs new homes, new schools, a new deal for older people, new industries and new opportunities for everyone

Britain needs a Labour Government

LET'S GO!

*Politics **can** be sold like detergents! The Conservative Party poster uses the advertiser's familiar device of offering something 'better' (better than what?). The Labour Party uses much the same language as the detergent which promises 'a square deal'.*

SPECIAL WITH SQUARE DEAL SURF...

SQUARE DEAL

Surf

GUARANTEED 1 lb 3 oz NET WEIGHT

ALWAYS MORE POWDER— MORE VALUE— MORE SHINING WHITENESS!

...A Square Deal!

That's what you get with Square Deal Surf— a simple, straightforward, value-for-money Square Deal! There's nothing with it that you don't want. No "free gifts", nothing to send away for, nothing in the packet but washing powder—extra powder you can use in your washing machine. Yes always 18% more top-quality powder than with any other leading detergent, for the same price—with the full weight *guaranteed*.

That's the Square Deal you get with Square Deal Surf!

GUARANTEED MORE POWDER FOR THE SAME PRICE—such good sense!

Don't ask a man to drink and drive

DANGER!
ADVERTISEMENT!

This is an advertisement for Whyte & Mackay's, the lightest-tasting Scotch whisky on sale today. This opens two possibilities: either you are influenced by advertisements or you are not. If you are not, then stop reading this and buy a bottle right away, so that you can find out all about it for yourself. On the other hand, if you do believe what advertisements say, then we shall be happy to inform you further: Whyte & Mackay's is not only, we repeat, the lightest-tasting Scotch whisky on sale today, it is also the cleanest-tasting, and most delicately blended. Moreover, it is one of the oldest proprietary brands. It inspired many Victorians to achieve greatness.

This still leaves you two possibilities: you either like light whisky, or you don't. If you don't, we are sorry to have wasted your time (and our money), but if you do, then you have only one possibility: you must buy a bottle of Whyte & Mackay's right away, and find out just how true this advertisement really is.

Picture shows: measure-capped bottle, glass, and owner thereof, all containing the lightest whisky you can buy—Whyte & Mackay's. Not lighter in strength, not lighter in colour, but lighter in taste. Available in bottles with the new measure cap, half and quarter pocket flasks and miniatures.

WHYTE & MACKAY LTD., GLASGOW (CENTRAL 4416) AND LONDON (TIDEWAY 6151)
An Independent Company Established 1844

Before you smoke THINK cigarettes cause lung cancer

Unlike much commercial advertising, propaganda offers slogans rather than information. The two posters (left) would hardly be more effective if they supported their messages with facts. But the whisky firm who use a warning to attract attention (incidentally turning the controversy about advertising to their advantage) back it up with detailed information.

give you lung cancer. In any case, facts alone are of little help to the consumer until he has tested goods or services for himself or formed a view of them from other people's experience. Insistence on nothing but 'factual' advertising (supposing it proved workable) might produce something more undesirable even than the silliest or most pernicious advertisement: direct censorship by an authoritarian body which would select or censor the 'facts'.

Moreover, people do not merely buy things for their functional or practical value. We do not buy suits and skirts just to cover our nakedness, or food simply to stave off hunger, or houses only to shelter us from the weather. With all such possessions we buy an intangible additional element: style, associations of comfort and gracefulness, the appeals of sophistication, design and culture. What are the 'facts' about these qualities?

The advertiser's message often carries with it an appeal to wit and discrimination. Some of this rubs off, as it were, on to the product itself. We would feel different sitting behind the wheel of a Jaguar from how we feel behind the wheel of a Ford. Or, to hark back to an earlier example, we feel different munching a box of Black Magic during Swan Lake at Covent Garden from dipping into our Maltesers on the pillion seat of the boy-friend's Lambretta. The physical pleasures may be roughly equal, but psychologically or emotionally they are *different*; and that difference – which has nothing to do with 'facts' or 'information' about the product – has been contributed by the advertiser.

The same applies to pills and medicines. In all proprietary brands, no doubt, there is a drug or palliative which brings some measure of relief. But a well-conceived advertisement is capable of giving a headache sufferer, say, more confidence in the product or feeling of relief than if he had used a rival brand. In this sense, the advertiser's claim that his remedy is 'quickest' or 'instant' may prove to be true, though no amount of chemical analysis could ever prove it.

We all know people who 'swear by' somebody's powders or somebody else's pills. They may be right, and these medicines may be – for them – the most effective medicines of their kind on the market; but it is impossible to draw a line between the intrinsic properties of the product and its effective value to the sufferer-believer. Or take cosmetics: if a girl is taken in by an advertisement that promises her she will look attractive if she wears a certain lipstick, she may very well look attractive simply because she *thinks* she looks attractive. Did the advertisement then tell a lie?

Advertising to young people

Here we are in the realms of the abstract, where psychology and suggestion take over from hard physical fact. But we also touch here on the fringe of the moral aspect of advertising, especially as it affects young people. The advertisers' assault on the young consumer is sometimes thought objectionable. Boys and girls on the verge of adulthood are exposed to the same 'hard-sell' values by means of which products are popularised in the adult market. Sex appeal and 'romance' are often promoted as being ends in themselves instead of – as in real life – aspects of much more broadly based, mature, social and personal behaviour. Such advertisements peddle dreams rather than reality. They present a simplified, idealised world in which we are all good-looking and well dressed and indulge our appetites as we please.

In this advertisers' dream-world the great thing is to be on the inside, 'with it' pretty or popular, untroubled by social problems and with ready-made remedies always on hand. It is a world in which housework is fun and children are winsome little angels. It bears as much relation to real life as a commercial jingle bears to Beethoven's Ninth Symphony.

This air of idealised unreality is most marked in the television commercials. From the outset, they had a revolutionary impact on mass marketing, largely because – perhaps for the first time in history – people found themselves actively *enjoying* advertisements. The most popular ones used the techniques and accent of show business: advertisers' jingles and comic catch-phrases passed briefly into the language. But television has not proved the most popular medium for advertising expensive products, notably motor cars. Perhaps the prevailing moods of the TV commercial, often inclining towards facetiousness or a glib 'sincerity', are partly to blame.

Questions

1. Take an issue of your favourite magazine and mark each displayed advertisement with the 'want' to which you think it is appealing. How many of the advertisements appeal to healthy tastes and instincts and how many to less worthy ones?

2. Do you think that 'keeping up with the Joneses' is a driving force in modern life? What are the arguments for and against?

3. Try to write a purely *factual* advertisement for (i) Player's cigarettes; (ii) Shell petrol; (iii) any brand of sweets or chocolates; (iv) a cosmetic or toothpaste; (v) a product aimed at your favourite hobby.

4. Find examples of advertisements which appeal mainly to (*a*) the snob instinct, (*b*) ambition. How do they do it?

5. Take examples of advertising by 'good causes' and non-commercial organisations (such as the armed forces) and discuss how they use the best and the most irritating features of commercial advertising.

5. Advertising—Foul or Fair?

ANY discussion of advertising leads sooner or later to a discussion of modern society in general. At the beginning of this short outline it was suggested that it is the outward and material aspect of daily life that gives the clue to the standard of living. But of course 'standard of living' is itself one of those phrases which beg half the questions. The standard of general prosperity can be measured. So, roughly, can the standard of comfort, cleanliness, medical care and all the other aspects of material welfare. But what of the other aspect; the *quality* of daily life?

It is at this point that a consideration of advertising and its functions becomes more general, and more controversial. Advertisers claim that their activities play a central part in advancing the economy by speeding the flow of goods and stepping up competition. But have they enough of a social conscience? Are they justified in using *all* means at their disposal to sell their goods, even at the expense of moral or cultural values which are themselves part of a well-developed 'standard of living'?

Insulting our intelligence

Of course they are not; and there are safeguards which try to ensure that the excesses of commercial pressure meet with prompt correction. We shall look at them in a moment. But there are a number of ways in which advertisers, without overtly breaking any law or any written code, debase our language and insult our intelligence.

Examples include the advertising of some useful but basically humdrum commodities in terms more appropriate to, say, liqueur chocolates. Some brands of toilet paper, for instance, are promoted in language which seeks to give the product an incongruous glamour: language written, *Private Eye* once put it, by people with 'soft, absorbent minds'. The language of many advertisements offends against both intelligence and syntax, such as the ad-man's unrelated comparative: 'whiter', 'cleaner', 'brighter' – than what?

These are points at which advertising lays itself open to criticism from teachers who see it as part of the mass culture which Professor Richard Hoggart[1] has described as 'anti-life', and which Mr. David Holbrook[2] attacks as being damaging to school-children's creative work. Most of us can put up some kind of resistance to the more blatant sales-talk, but subtler messages may well get through. One way of checking such claims might be to give advertisers freedom to 'knock' one another's products – 'knock' in this context being trade jargon for denigrate or disparage. Some advertisers come near to it in rather muted ways: the wool industry, for instance, hits obliquely at man-made fibres, nationalised railways hit at road transport, and the butter makers at margarine.

This was one of the aspects of advertising investigated by the Government-appointed Committee on Consumer Protection – known as the Molony Committee – whose Report in 1962 included suggestions for various reforms. On the 'knocking

[1] In *The Uses of Literacy*, 1957.
[2] In *The Secret Places*, 1964.

TABLE VII

TOP FIFTEEN ADVERTISING AGENCIES IN 1967

(£ million to nearest £100,000)

	Agency	Total £m	T.V. %	Press %	Total Billings in 1963[1] £m
1	J. Walter Thompson	17·62	75	25	16·1
2	Masius, Wynne-Williams	15·37	74	26	12·8
2	London Press Exchange	11·97	67	33	22·4
4	Ogilvy & Mather	10·52	56	44	13·1
5	S. H. Benson	10·50	59	41	27·9
6	Hobson Bates & Partners	8·74	69	31	6·5
7	Young & Rubicam	8·71	81	19	7·4
8	Lintas	7·51	85	15	3·4
9	Erwin Wasey	5·82	63	37	8·9
10	Foote, Cone & Belding	5·38	62	38	5·9
11	Dorland Advertising	5·19	62	38	5·4
12	G. S. Royds	4·95	52	48	4·9
13	McCann Erickson	4·86	64	36	6·8
14	Collett Dickinson & Pearce	4·40	40	60	2·57
15	Pritchard Wood & Partners	4·20	70	30	9·3

Source: Media Expenditure Analysis Ltd.

[1]*Advertising Age*, 2 March 1964. These figures include billings in offices outside Britain. Billings are the total of sums spent on advertising by agents on behalf of their clients.

N.B: Wholly-owned subsidiary agencies and associated companies have been included with their parent companies.

If you were chairman of a small agency with total billings of £500,000 what thoughts would you have if you were offered a new account which promised total billings of a further £500,000? Would you accept the account? Give your reasons.

---

copy' issue, however, it felt that people are sensible enough to know that advertisers' claims do not necessarily establish the comparative worth of their products. On the whole, they said, they preferred this state of affairs to the consumer being confused by efforts to rationalise and justify competing claims. But some economists have argued in favour of knocking copy. And the first chairman of the Advertising Standards Authority, Professor Sir Arnold Plant (himself a distinguished economist), has urged the advertising industry to consider it.

Complaints against advertising

But modern methods of advertising do arouse disquiet in many quarters. One complaint put to the Molony Committee was that advertising has abandoned any serious attempt to inform the public, and hammers home its message so relentlessly that the consumer finds himself buying on the strength of an instinctive, almost hypnotised reaction to the brand name. Again, the Committee were told that advertisers make meaningless claims, or that their products contain some special ingredient with a pseudo-technical name, or that they play on the fears of people such as a mother's fear of failing in her duty to her family, or a general fear of unpopularity.

The Molony Report 'regretted' the departure from factual advertising and the increase in high-pressure 'brand image' advertising, but saw it as an inevitable result of mass marketing. As for the charge that advertisers make misleadingly vague claims, what (asked the Committee) is a 'reasonable' inference, and what is 'undue' exaggeration? It did not feel qualified to say. Similarly with the claims made for a new constituent: if it has been described with reasonable accuracy, the advertiser is not, in the Committee's view, to be blamed though in some cases 'it may pass into the realm of the objectionable.'

On appeals to fear, however, the Committee were more definite: 'It would not disturb us if a manufacturer of flame-resistant children's nightwear indulged in advertising to shock parents. . . . At the other extreme, we have viewed with disgust an advertisement in which a manufacturer of toilet paper deliberately played on fear of poliomyelitis.' Summing up on advertising, the Molony Report found that a potential harm to the consumer does exist and that there is a need to restrain it.

Disciplines and detergents

But there is already a point at which the advertiser's temptation to go all out in his emotional or psychological assault on the public runs into opposition, both from the law of the land and from professional codes of conduct.

The consumer is protected against people who seek to sell him things by falsehoods or subterfuge. As long ago as 1887 the first Merchandising Act imposed penalties on traders found guilty of applying false trade descriptions to goods. The Sale of Goods Act in 1893 strengthened that law and gave the customer redress against traders who sold goods that proved defective or unsuitable to their declared purpose. More recently, the Merchandising Marks Act of 1953 extended the term 'trade description' to cover any indication of the quality of the goods, their performance, strength or fitness for the purpose for which they were sold or advertised. Under that Act, too, it became a punishable offence to include misleading descriptions – not merely false ones. Now, following the Molony Report, some further tightening up is likely and the Consumer Council was set up in 1963 to co-ordinate the various ways of protecting the customer.

Again, an organisation called the Retail Trading Standards Association, and some newspaper groups, have long acted as watchdogs in the shopkeeper's interest. The advertising profession itself has developed codes of practice, with powers (not used often enough) to keep offending advertisements from appearing a second time. (There was an example in 1962 of how one such body, the British Poster Advertising Association, turned its code of propriety against the Government: it banned a Ministry of Health poster bearing the slogan 'Cigarettes Cause Lung Cancer' as being unfairly exaggerated.)

The consumer is therefore protected by law, by information and by independent advice. He is also in some measure protected by bodies devoted to censoring, or in some cases forbidding, certain advertisements, though here it is difficult to distinguish between objective vigilance and political self-interest. The total apparatus of protection is, nevertheless, on the increase. It includes codes of conduct laid down by the various advertisers' associations for the guidance of their members; and the Advertising Standards Authority keeps an eye – though not, perhaps, an all-seeing one – on offenders.

The ultimate protection—common sense

But probably the most powerful force of all is the common sense and intelligence of ordinary men and women, in a society where each is free to make his own choice. Consumers – which in this context is only another word for people – are generally more wordly-wise than sociologists imagine. In a healthy democracy, people should be encouraged to be more and more aware – even sceptical – of persuasion in all its forms. But it would be defeating the ends of democracy if, having rid the advertising industry of its abuses, we installed a brand of political persuasion in its place.

Ultimately it is people, housewives, shoppers of every kind, who exercise the one control that matters: control over their own expenditure and therefore – given choice and competition – over the fortunes of all who seek to sell them good, indifferent or bad products by equally varied means. To deny this is to deny the citizen the right to spend his money where and how he likes. It is permissible to deplore some of the ways in which he may spend his money, but it is intolerant to try and deprive him of the right to choose.

It is in many ways depressing that so many people fail to make the most of the abundant choices that were once the privilege of the wealthy alone. Instead, in the first flush of popular prosperity, many people seem to want the same sort of product and to share exactly the same tastes. This leads to conformity of a kind which agitates some commentators who see the nation developing into a faceless 'Admass'. For this, advertising gets much of the blame. Even here there is a danger of confusing cause and effect. Is it an effect of advertising that most people choose to live in the same kind of house, drive the same sort of car, wash up in the same kind of soap powder, wear the same kind of clothes and speak with the same kind of accent? Or is there not a deep-seated instinct in many of us to live like other people, to take our ideas and values from society as a whole? (And, of course, it is much cheaper to buy what many others buy than to have exclusive, bespoke clothes, cars or cat food.)

In any case, there can be no one more conformist than a peasant in a backward country, with no chance to express what spark of individuality may be in him by dressing differently, or furnishing his home with Swedish chairs instead of uncut moquette, or standing a piece of abstract sculpture in his front garden (if he has one) instead of a little fishing gnome. At least in our own society the choice is there: you can conform or not. Within limits, it's up to you.

Advertisers who need to sell their wares in the mass market have to address us collectively. They make the kind of appeal which they think will be most effective to a *majority*; and in doing so they irritate, offend, bore or exasperate sizeable minorities. These minorities in their turn may be catered for by more selective advertisers, or they can disregard advertisements altogether if they have a mind to. A purist whose antagonism to mass production with its enormous economies and mass marketing carried him to logical extremes would live in a home-made house in clothes he had made and designed himself (perhaps no clothes at all) and feed, as his ancestors did, off berries and roots.

A lead from minorities

Our society has not yet reached the point where every individual human want or desire can be instantly satisfied; it is doubtful indeed, if such a state of affairs is desirable. But a rising standard of living does bring with it the *means* to satisfy more and more personal wants and desires, and as discrimination becomes general so manufacturers pay increasing attention to minority wants. These in turn become more widely popular as general demand catches up with them, and as the means to provide them – meaning incomes or wealth – becomes more and more widely distributed. As a direct result, standards of design rise as the wishes of the discriminating minority become in time the accepted standards of a majority: a process one can already see at work in the design of houses, furniture and domestic equipment of every kind, and which as time goes by may spread to taste in literature, music, television, education, welfare, holidays and many aspects of family life.

Discrimination can never be a characteristic of the mass market, but the mass market itself may in future break up into sections, each of which will command the separate attention of manufacturers and advertisers. As has been remarked earlier, it is seldom easy to be sure where human wants begin and the advertisers' hunches take over. But wherever the distinction may be found, the market for goods and services depends on people being interested and wanting to buy. The manufacturer looking for a 'gimmick' to help sell a new product, or to revive the fortunes of an existing one, is in very much the same situation as the politician casting round for a policy, panacea, or a 'message' to persuade the electorate to vote his way. There is no absolutely certain means of telling in advance what people want or how they will choose. This may be frustrating to advertisers, market researchers and politicians, but it is a reassurance to the rest of us.

Not even the most brilliant advertisement will sell an inferior product for long. This truth applies equally to commerce and, in a non-totalitarian society, to politics as well. Given a free choice, people will come to use it with increasing care and intelligence. The monopolist who thinks he can shout or bully his way through is in much the same position as the dictator who harangues the crowd from a balcony. Neither cuts a dignified or civilised figure.

Advertising is not in itself either a wasteful or an undesirable product of the society we have built for ourselves. It is an inseparable part of a system which, taken as a whole, is bringing benefits to men and women on a scale never dreamed of in past times. To keep a fresh and informed mind about it is to keep it firmly in its place as an instrument of an economy in which men are working, however imperfectly, towards a better life.

Questions

1. Find examples of advertisements which 'give a product a spurious glamour'. Are these offensive, harmless or just silly?

2. Discuss the pros and cons of introducing additional safeguards in the publication of advertisements.

3. Do you agree that 'many people want the same sort of product and to share exactly the same tastes'? Discuss this as a main cause of the trend towards uniformity, as opposed to commercial pressures in the mass market.

4. Minority taste in house design and furniture has spread to a wider public, to the general benefit. How far has advertising helped in this process? Can you think of other examples?

5. Does the existence of advertising support the charge that we live in a purely materialistic society?

6. Why do you think most advertising seems to be for consumption goods or services and relatively little for welfare services or cultural activities?

Further Reading

Baynes, Michael, *Advertising on Trial*. Bow Group, 1956.

Bishop, F. P., *The Economics of Advertising*. Robert Hale, 1944. *The Ethics of Advertising*. Robert Hale, 1949.

Borden, N. H., *The Economic Effects of Advertising*. Irwin, Chicago, 1942.

Brown, J. A. C., *Techniques of Persuasion*. Penguin Books, 1963.

Dichter, Ernest, *The Strategy of Desire*. Boardman, 1960.

Economists Advisory Group, *Economics of Advertising*. The Advertising Association, 1967.

Final Report of the Committee on Consumer Protection (The Molony Report). HMSO, 1962.

Galbraith, J. K., *The Affluent Society*. Hamish Hamilton, 1958.

Gundrey, Elizabeth, *Your Money's Worth*. Penguin Books, March 1962.

Harris, Ralph & Seldon, Arthur, *Advertising & the Public*. Institute of Economic Affairs, 1962. *Advertising in Action*. Institute of Economic Affairs, 1962.

Hoggart, Richard, *The Uses of Literacy*. Chatto & Windus, 1957.

Holbrook, David, *The Secret Places*. Longmans, 1964.

Leavis, F. R., & Thompson, Denys, *Culture & Environment*. Chatto & Windus, 1933.

Mayer, Martin, *Madison Avenue, USA*. The Bodley Head, 1958.

NUT, *The Teacher Looks at Advertising*, May 1963.

Packard, Vance, *The Hidden Persuaders*. Longmans, 1957. *The Waste Makers*. Penguin Books, 1963.

PEP, *Consumer Protection and Enlightenment*, Vol. XXVI, No. 441, 25 April 1960.

Sawers, David, Altman, Wilfred, & Thomas, Denis, *TV: From Monopoly to Competition – and Back?* (Second Edition). Hobart Paper 15, Institute of Economic Affairs, 1962.

Taplin, Walter, 'Advertising Appropriation Policy'. *Economica*, August 1959. *Advertising – a New Approach*. Hutchinson, 1960. *The Origin of Television Advertising in the United Kingdom*. Pitman, 1961.

Telser, Lester G., *Advertising and Competition*. Occasional Paper 4, Institute of Economic Affairs, May 1965.

Thomas, Denis, *The Visible Persuaders*. Hutchinson, 1967.

Turner, E. S., *The Shocking History of Advertising*. Michael Joseph, 1952.

Williams, Francis (now Lord Francis-Williams), *Dangerous Estate*. Longmans, 1957. *The American Invasion*. Blond, 1962.